When I was a baby...
by Kelley Wotherspoon
Illustrated by J. Adam Farster

ISBN: 978-0-9990188-0-4

First Edition

Printed in the United States of America

Copyright © 2017 by Kelley Wotherspoon . All rights reserved. Any resemblance to actual persons living or dead, businesses, events or locales is purely coincidental. Reproduction in whole or part without the express written consent is strictly prohibited.

When I was a baby . . . is dedicated to my two beautiful children who keep me on my toes every day with their humorous wit, mischievous antics and barrage of hugs and kisses that make each moment sweeter than the last, to my amazing husband who has encouraged and supported me throughout this entire process and to my Gramps who believed in my writing from the moment I was able to scribble down words on a page.

When I was a baby,
did you feed me a bottle?

I did!
I fed you a bottle and hummed you a tune
Late into the night as we smiled at the moon.

When I was a baby,
did you burp me?

I did!
I patted your back and snuggled you close,
Rubbed your full tummy and tickled your toes.

When I was a baby,
did you change my diaper?

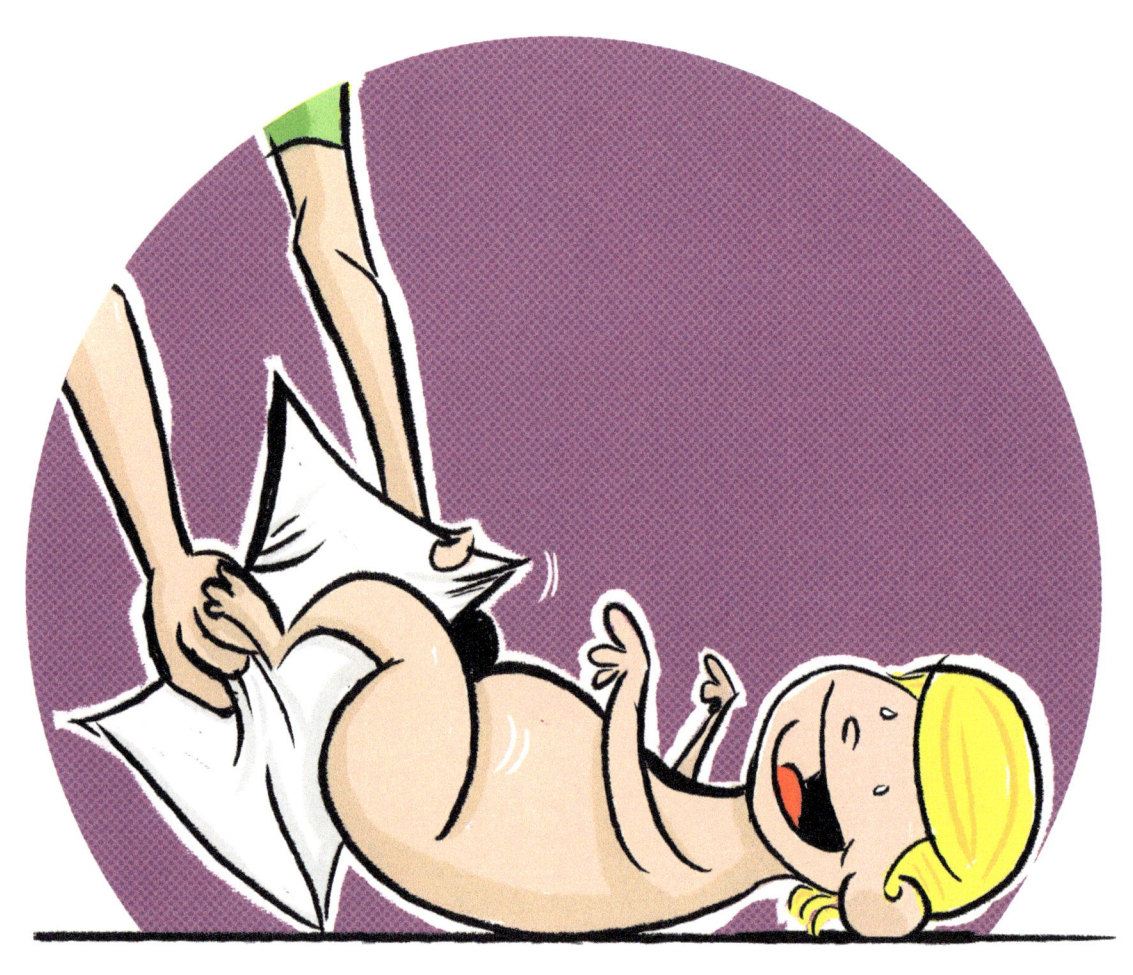

I did!
I changed your diaper with loving hands
Around wiggly legs not ready to stand.

When I was a baby,
did you give me a bath?

I did!
I washed you with bubbles that danced all about
As you splashed and you giggled
and you let out a shout.

When I was a baby, did you dress me in little clothes?

I did!
I picked out your outfits so tiny and sweet,
Put hats on your head and shoes on your feet.

When I was a baby,
did you rock me to sleep?

I did!
I hugged you and rocked you and kissed you goodnight,
Watched your bright eyes close slowly and held you so tight.

When I was a baby,
did you love me?

I did!
I loved you so much and I always will,
I loved you back then and I'm loving you still!

CPSIA information can be obtained
at www.ICGtesting.com
Printed in the USA
LVOW05s1950170717
541697LV00010B/225/P